# Discovering Earthquakes and Volcanoes

Written by Laura Damon

Illustrated by John R. Jones

**Troll Associates**

*Library of Congress Cataloging-in-Publication Data*

Damon, Laura.
    Discovering earthquakes and volcanoes / by Laura Damon;
illustrated by John R. Jones.
        p.    cm.
    Summary: An introduction to earthquakes and their causes, and to
the formation and eruptions of volcanoes.
    ISBN 0-8167-1757-5 (lib. bdg.)        ISBN 0-8167-1758-3 (pbk.)
    1. Earthquakes—Juvenile literature.    2. Volcanoes—Juvenile
literature.    [1. Earthquakes.    2. Volcanoes.]    I. Jones, John R.,
ill.    II. Title.
QE521.3.D36    1990
551.2—dc20                                                                89-4974

Copyright © 1990 by Troll Associates

For one hundred twenty-three years, a giant slept. That giant was a mountain in the state of Washington—a volcano named Mount St. Helens.

Then in March 1980, an earthquake rumbled. Mount St. Helens shook. The giant was about to awaken.

In the days after that, one earthquake followed another. Bits of ash and steam began to blow from the top of the volcano. A giant bulge also was growing beneath the rocks on one side of the mountaintop.

At last, on May 18, Mount St. Helens blew its top. The volcano erupted. This means that the heat, gases, and melted rock, called magma, inside the mountain came bursting out.

An avalanche of sliding snow moved down the mountain. It tore open the bulge that had grown on the top of the volcano.

A giant blast of steam burst through the hole in the
mountain. Steam is water that has turned to a gas by becoming
very, very hot. The steam blast was like a hot, strong wind,
and it carried a huge amount of rock and dirt into the air.

Moving with great force, the blowing rocks knocked down
whole forests as if they were toothpicks. And still, the volcano
was not done. It kept on erupting, filling the air with big
clouds of black ash and smoky gas. For miles around, the sky
turned dark.

When the volcano was quiet at last, fifty-seven people had died. The mighty volcano had also destroyed countless animals and plants.

Volcanoes and earthquakes are two of nature's worst disasters. But what causes them?

Long ago, people believed these disasters were caused by the gods. In fact, the word volcano comes from "Vulcan," the god of fire in ancient Rome.

Today, scientists know that earthquakes and volcanoes happen when pressures and forces inside the earth move the rocks that make up the earth's surface.

In a volcano, magma, the red-hot melted rock inside the earth, pushes up to the earth's surface. Hot gases, pieces of rock, and lava blast through an opening in the earth. Lava is the name given to magma after it comes out of the volcano.

During an earthquake, the earth's surface shakes, trembles, and often breaks apart. This happens because the rocks below the surface have been stretched or squeezed so hard that they finally snap! The snapping rocks move against one another like falling dominoes, making the earth shake.

Terrible though they are, volcanoes and earthquakes help us to understand what lies below the earth's surface. Do you know what the inside of the earth is like? Geologists, scientists who study the earth, have many ideas about the inside of the earth. They believe that if you could cut the earth in half, like an apple, you would see four main layers inside.

The outer layer is the earth's *crust*. The oceans and the large pieces of land that make up the earth's surface are found on the crust.

Below the crust is a layer called the *mantle*. Magma is in the mantle. This melted rock is like a thick, hot paste, and it moves about.

Next come the *outer core* and *inner core* of the earth. Within the core, it is very, very hot. Scientists think the outer core is liquid and the inner core is solid.

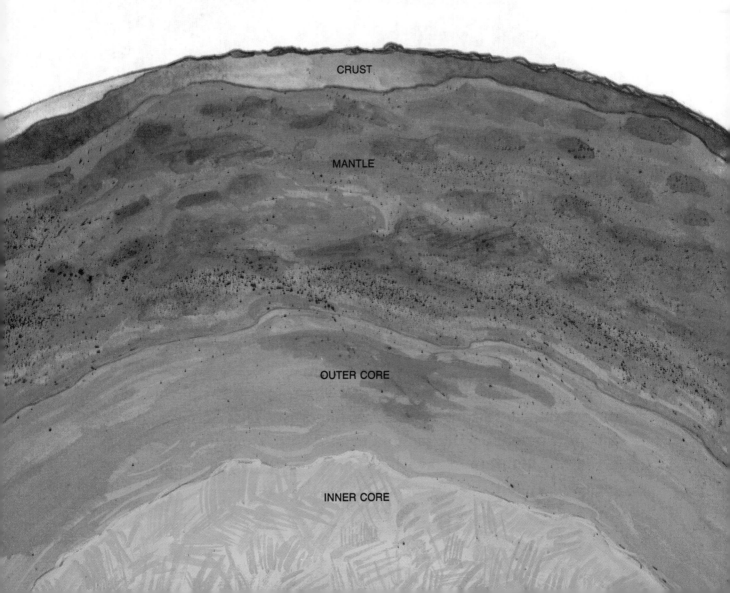

CRUST

MANTLE

OUTER CORE

INNER CORE

When a volcano erupts, the magma in the earth's mantle pushes its way through a hole in the crust. This hole is called a *vent*. Sometimes the magma erupts with great force, sending a red-hot fountain of lava high into the air. Other times, the lava slowly but steadily oozes out of the vent.

Bits and pieces of rock also erupt from a volcano. Some of these bits are very small—they form ash and dust. Other pieces of rock are much larger. They are called *volcanic bombs* and may be more than four feet (1 m) wide.

The gas that pours out of a volcano is made mostly of steam, plus some other gases. The steam often looks like dark smoke because it carries ash and dust.

There are three different kinds of volcanoes. Each has a special shape.

The first kind is called a *cinder cone.* As its name says, this volcano looks like a giant cone. A cinder-cone volcano is made when cinders—bits of dust, ash, and rock—erupt from the vent. These cinders settle all around the volcano. They form a cone.

*Shield* volcanoes erupt in a different way. Very liquid lava flows freely from the volcano's hole. The lava spreads far out around the volcano, making a mountain with a low, broad dome.

CINDER CONE

COMPOSITE VOLCANO

The third kind of volcano is called a *composite* volcano. The word composite means "put together with special parts"— and that is just how this volcano is made. Both lava and bits of rock and dust erupt. These materials form layer upon layer around the volcano's hole. Little by little, the layers grow into a tall, towerlike mountain. Two famous examples of composite volcanoes are Vesuvius in Italy and pretty Mount Fuji in Japan.

SHIELD VOLCANO

Most volcanoes take place in an area of the world called the Ring of Fire. Named for its many volcanoes, the Ring of Fire makes a sort of circle around the Pacific Ocean. Other volcanoes often erupt below the sea along chains of underwater mountains. Still other volcanoes erupt in Iceland, southern Europe, and Hawaii.

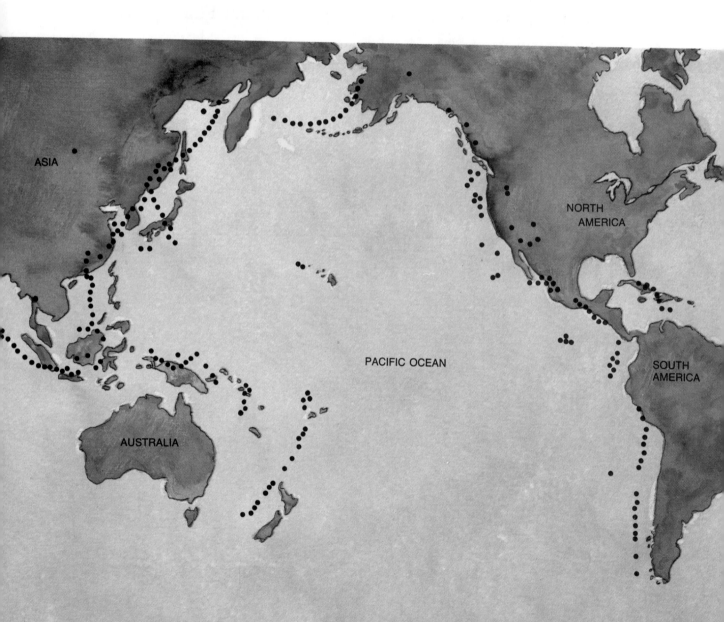

Some volcanoes destroy land, but others actually make new land. In 1963, people watched from the coast of Iceland as a volcano erupted in the ocean. Bit by bit, the lava around the volcano grew higher until a brand-new island appeared above the water. The new island was named Surtsey.

Geologists watched Surtsey carefully to see what would happen. They found that in only two years' time, the island was already the home of many birds, insects, and plants.

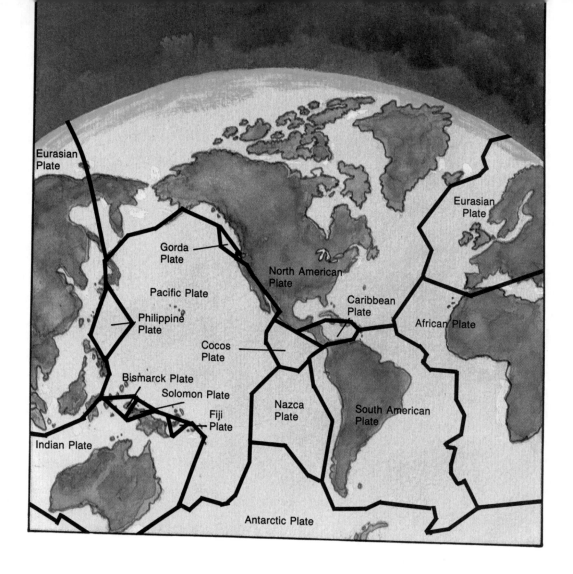

Eurasian Plate

Eurasian Plate

Gorda Plate

North American Plate

Pacific Plate

Caribbean Plate

African Plate

Philippine Plate

Cocos Plate

Bismarck Plate

Solomon Plate

Fiji Plate

Nazca Plate

South American Plate

Indian Plate

Antarctic Plate

Why do most volcanoes take place only in certain parts of the world, such as the Ring of Fire? Geologists have a theory, or idea, why this happens.

They believe the earth's outer crust is made up of many huge sections of rock. Each section is called a *plate*. Like a giant jigsaw puzzle, the plates roughly fit together. But the plates do not stay still. They are always moving. The plates move because they float upon the magma that lies below them.

As the plates move, several things may happen along their edges. For example, when two plates hit into one another, one plate may be forced beneath the other plate. The tremendous rubbing between the two plates creates heat. The heat melts rock into magma. The magma then rises to the earth's surface, and a volcano is born.

Magma

The edges of two plates may also move apart, leaving a
space. When this happens, magma may move up into the space,
and again, a volcano erupts.

Ocean

Ocean Floor

Magma

In some cases, two plates may slide past one another. A place where this happens is called a *fault*. Most faults are under the earth's surface, but there is one that can be clearly seen. It is in the United States in California. It is called the San Andreas fault. Here, the edges of two plates are sliding past one another, and the deep ridge between them can be seen. It looks like a long crack or scar on the earth's surface.

Earthquakes often happen along faults. Here is why: The rubbing of two plates causes a great force. If the force is too great, the rocks that make up the plates cannot stretch anymore. The rocks break apart, causing an earthquake.

As the built-up pressure in the snapping rocks is set free, the rocks bump against one another, and the earth shakes. Think of how a tightly pulled rubber band snaps and then shakes when it is let go. Something like that happens during an earthquake, only in a much larger way.

The shaking motion of an earthquake travels through the earth in waves. A wave is sort of like a push. The damage caused by these waves can be very great in a big quake.

Scientists have found that there are about one million earthquakes every year. Luckily, most are very small. Also many earthquakes take place beneath the sea, so they do no damage.

When a big earthquake takes place near a city, many lives may be lost. Buildings crumble and fall. Fires, sometimes caused by fallen wires, rage out of control.

Perhaps one of the most frightening effects of an earthquake is the *tsunami*, or tidal wave. This Japanese word describes a giant sea wave caused by the movement of the earthquake. The tsunami rises high and sweeps up upon the land, destroying everything in its path.

To study and measure volcanoes and earthquakes, scientists use special tools. With these tools, they hope to be able to predict these natural disasters in order to save lives.

For studying both volcanoes and earthquakes, a machine called a *seismograph* is used. It measures the waves given off during earthquakes.

Geologists measure the strength of an earthquake with something called the Richter scale, which is named after its inventor, Charles F. Richter. The scale is based on measurements of waves or vibrations, called *seismic waves*, given off by earthquakes. Any quake that measures 6 or higher on the Richter scale is a big one.

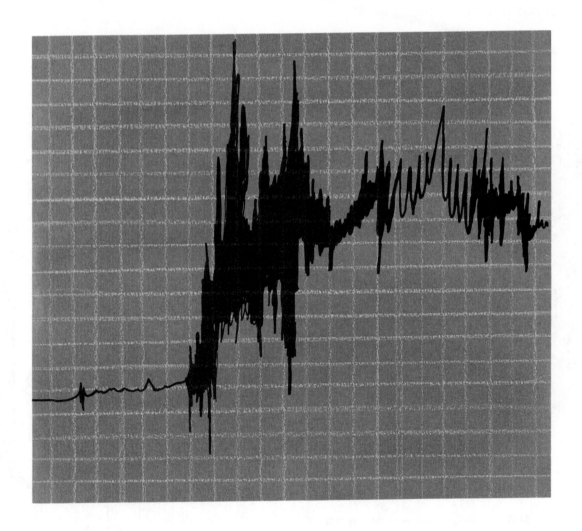

Special machines, such as gas detectors and thermometers, are useful in studying the changes in a volcano as it gets ready to erupt. Scientists also use a *tiltmeter*, a tool to measure a growing bulge of rock on a volcano, such as the one that formed on Mount St. Helens.

So far, geologists still cannot predict every volcano or earthquake. But they go on with their work, always hoping to become more exact.

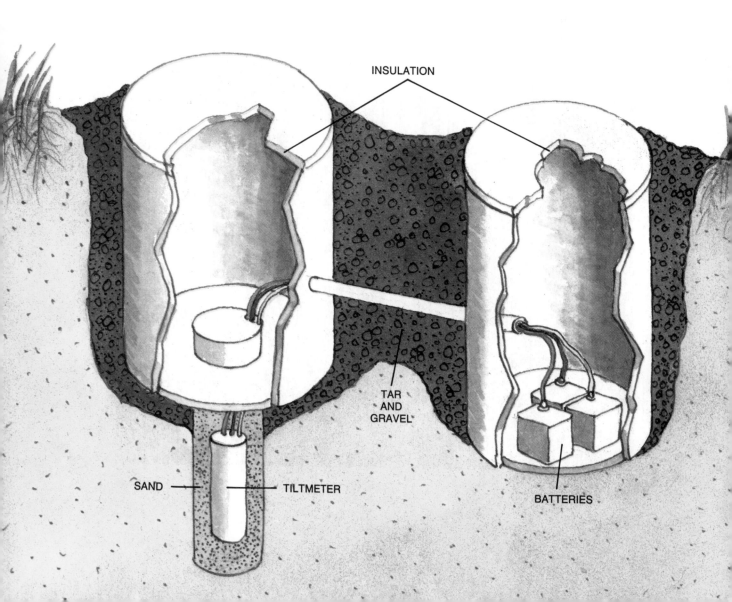

Volcanoes and earthquakes show us the great might of nature. And although they are destructive, volcanoes do have certain good effects. Gases and ash from volcanoes recycle minerals and other elements. The ash from a volcano also makes very rich soil.

But perhaps the greatest importance of earthquakes and volcanoes is that they show us how our earth is made. They help us look inside our earth. And finding the answers to our mysterious earth is one of our greatest challenges.